A LOOK AT WORLD HISTORY

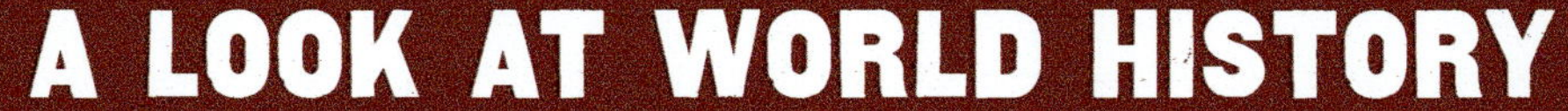

THE CRUSADES

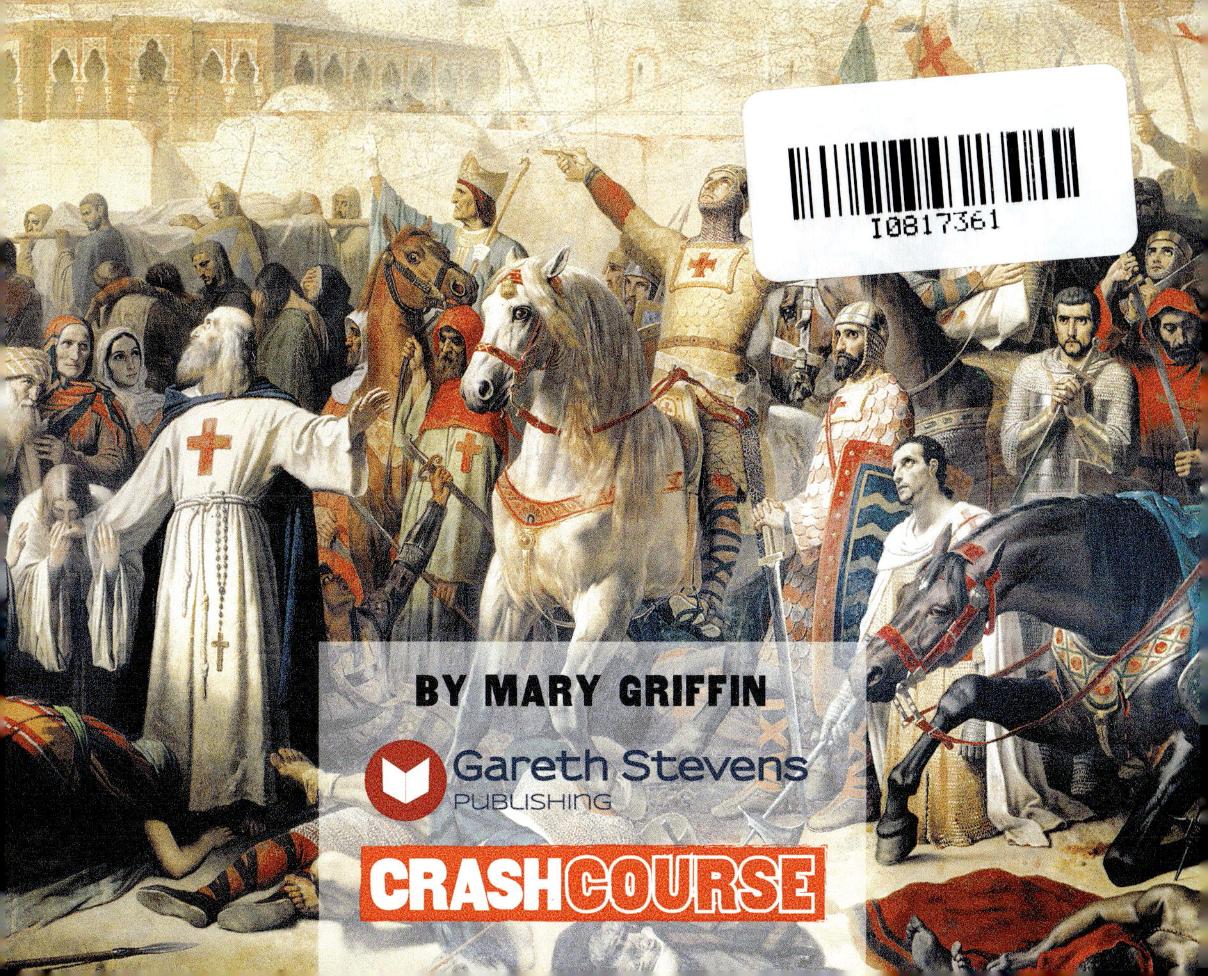

BY MARY GRIFFIN

Gareth Stevens PUBLISHING

CRASHCOURSE

Please visit our website, www.garethstevens.com. For a free color catalog of all our high-quality books, call toll free 1-800-542-2595 or fax 1-877-542-2596.

Library of Congress Cataloging-in-Publication Data

Names: Griffin, Mary, 1978- author.
Title: The Crusades / Mary Griffin.
Description: New York : Gareth Stevens Publishing, 2020. | Series: A look at world history | Includes index.
Identifiers: LCCN 2018039204| ISBN 9781538241349 (pbk.) | ISBN 9781538241363 (library bound) | ISBN 9781538241356 (6 pack)
Subjects: LCSH: Crusades--Juvenile literature.
Classification: LCC D157 .G65 2020 | DDC 909.07--dc23
LC record available at https://lccn.loc.gov/2018039204

First Edition

Published in 2020 by
Gareth Stevens Publishing
111 East 14th Street, Suite 349
New York, NY 10003

Designer: Katelyn E. Reynolds
Editor: Therese Shea

Photo credits: Cover, pp. 1, 15, 17 Leemage/Corbis via Getty Images; cover, pp. 1–32 (background) javarman/Shutterstock.com; cover, pp. 1–32 (border) Anastasiia Smiian/Shutterstock.com; p. 5 (inset) JekLi/Shutterstock.com; p. 5 (map) Andrei Minsk/Shutterstock.com; pp. 7, 9 Universal History Archive/UIG via Getty Images; p. 11 (Alexius I) GifTagger/Wikipedia.org; p. 11 (Pope Urban II) (https://archive.org/details/thelivesandtimes00montuoft)/Bede735c/Wikipedia.org; pp. 13, 29 Fine Art Images/Heritage Images/Getty Images; pp. 19 (Saladin), 27 Prisma/UIG/Getty Images; p. 19 (Conrad III) Scanned from *Die Zeit der Staufer*, Stuttgart 1977, vol. II, Abb. 544 (Kat. Nr. 752); cropped by Rosenzweig/ 竹麦魚 (Searobin)/Wikipedia.org; pp. 19 (King Louis VII), 25 Hulton Archive/Getty Images; p. 21 Historica Graphica Collection/Heritage Images/Getty Images; p. 23 Eugene Delacroix/Getty Images.

Printed in the United States of America

CPSIA compliance information: Batch #CS19GS: For further information contact Gareth Stevens, New York, New York at 1-800-542-2595.

CONTENTS

Words in the glossary appear in **bold** type the first time they are used in the text.

HOLY CITY IN THE HOLY LAND

The city of Jerusalem is holy to several **religions**. Christians believe it's where Jesus died and rose again. It's home to the Western Wall, a holy place where Jews pray. Muslims believe the **prophet** Muhammad was carried to heaven from Jerusalem.

MAKE THE GRADE

Some call Jerusalem the "holy city" and the land surrounding it—sometimes called Palestine—the "Holy Land."

Jerusalem was under mainly Muslim control from the 600s to the early 1900s. From the late 1000s to the 1200s, Christians began several wars against Muslims to **capture** the city and other parts of the Holy Land. These wars were called the Crusades.

ARTIST'S IDEA OF ANCIENT JERSUSALEM

MAKE THE GRADE

The word "crusade" wasn't used until the 1700s. It came from the French word *croisade*, and that came from the Latin word *crux*, meaning "cross." Christian soldiers often wore a cross into battle.

WHY WAR?

In the **Middle Ages**, many European rulers, as well as the Catholic Church, worried about the **expansion** of Muslim territory and the spread of the religion of Islam. They hoped war would stop this expansion and gain land for Christians.

MAKE THE GRADE

When the Crusades took place, Muslims controlled land from India to Spain. This area was sometimes called the califate.

In the 11th century, Muslims called Seljuq (SEHL-jook) Turks **conquered** parts of the Byzantine Empire. They captured Jerusalem and stopped Christians from entering the city. Byzantine emperor Alexius I asked the head of the Catholic Church, Pope Urban II, for help.

MAKE THE GRADE

The Byzantine Empire is another name for the Eastern Roman Empire. In the 11th century, it stretched from eastern Europe to Asia Minor.

THE FIRST CRUSADE

In 1095, Pope Urban II ordered Christians to capture Jerusalem. He promised soldiers that their sins would be forgiven if they fought in the war, later called the First Crusade. Others fought for land. Poor people called serfs fought because they were promised freedom.

MAKE THE GRADE

During the Middle Ages, Europeans lived under the feudal system. Lords and kings owned the land. Knights fought for them in return for land. Serfs were forced to serve those in power.

Many lives were lost on both sides during the **siege** of the city of Antioch, which is in Turkey today. Illness and hunger killed many as well. The Christians finally captured Antioch and then defeated, or beat, another siege by an army of Turks.

MAKE THE GRADE

Frenchman Peter Bartholomew claimed he found a lance that had wounded Jesus on the cross. This made Christians believe God was on their side in the battle against the Turks.

The Christian army traveled on to Jerusalem and captured it on July 15, 1099. After the victory, the Crusaders killed hundreds of Muslims and Jews who lived in the city, including women and children. Some said the streets were red with blood.

THE CAPTURE OF JERUSALEM, 1099

MAKE THE GRADE

An army of poor people and knights went on the People's Crusade in 1096, led by a powerful preacher named Peter the Hermit. However, the Turks easily defeated this force.

THE SECOND CRUSADE

Another war was called in 1145 to stop the spread of Muslim power. Emperor Conrad III of Germany and King Louis VII of France led the Second Crusade. The Crusaders were defeated. Under a leader named Saladin, Muslims recaptured Jerusalem in 1187.

MAKE THE GRADE

Special orders of knights guarded parts of the Holy Land, including the Knights Templars and the Teutonic Knights.

THE THIRD CRUSADE

The Third Crusade was called in 1189. Its leaders were Philip Augustus of France, Richard the Lion-Hearted of England, and Frederick I of Germany, also called Frederick Barbarossa. It had some success, winning the city of Acre in the Holy Land.

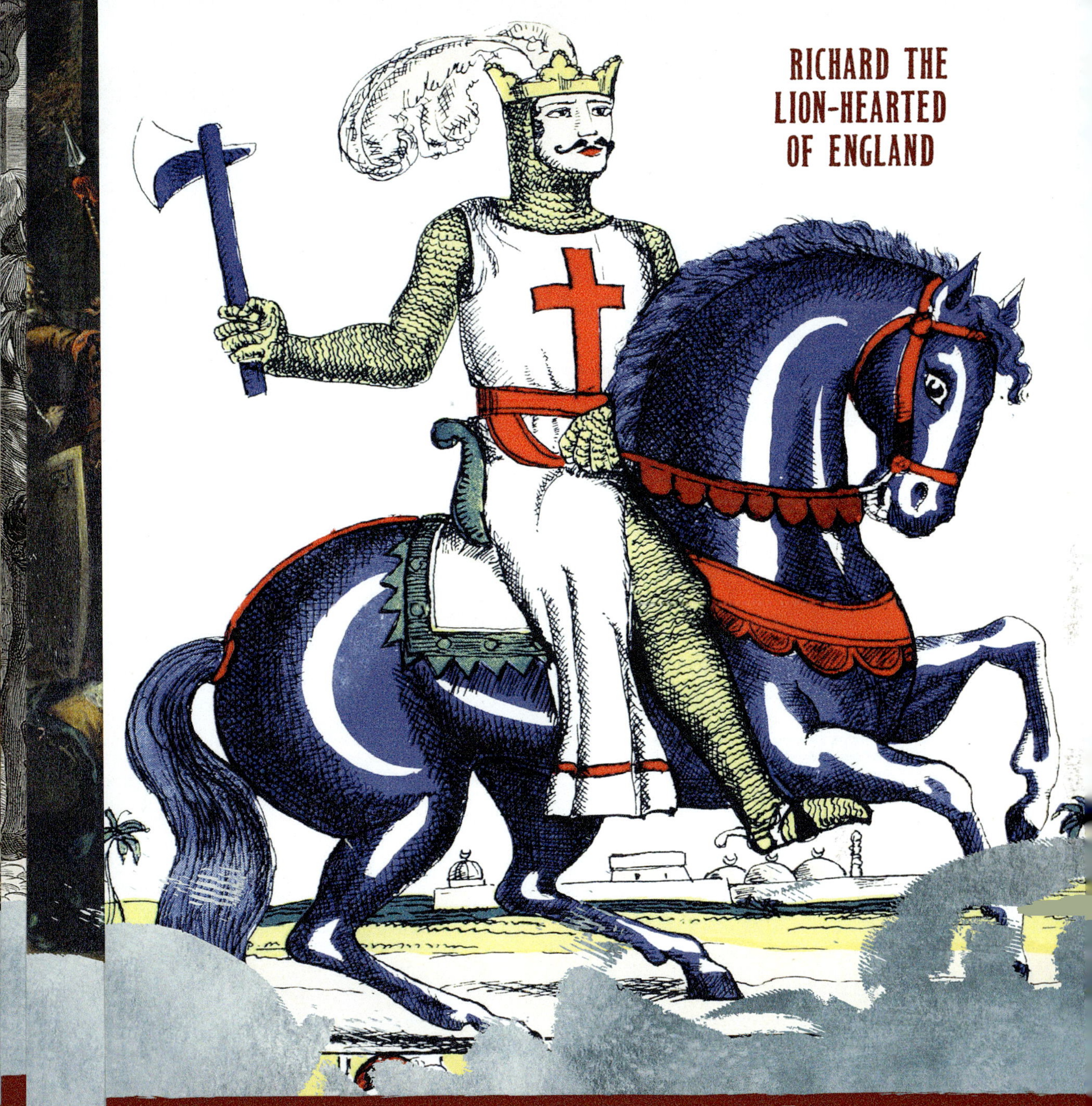

MAKE THE GRADE

Though the Crusaders couldn't recapture Jerusalem, King Richard and Saladin agreed Christians could visit certain holy places within the city for 3 years.

THE FOURTH CRUSADE

In 1198, Pope Innocent III called for a new crusade. The aim was to capture Egypt, an important area in the Muslim world. However, Christians turned against each other. In 1204, the Crusaders captured Constantinople, the capital of the Byzantine Empire.

MAKE THE GRADE

The Byzantines later recaptured Constantinople, but the Crusades had weakened the empire. It finally fell to the Ottoman Turks in 1453.

THE CHILDREN'S CRUSADE

Around 1212, a young German named Nicholas of Cologne gathered a group of children and poor people to fight in the Holy Land. However, Pope Innocent III told them to go home. Many never returned to Germany. Some were sold into slavery.

MAKE THE GRADE

In 1212, another group of young Crusaders gathered under the leadership of a French shepherd boy named Stephen. However, King Philip Augustus wouldn't allow these children to travel to the Holy Land to fight.

OTHER CRUSADES

In 1218, the Fifth Crusade began. It took soldiers to Egypt but failed. The emperor of the **Holy Roman Empire**, Frederick II, called the Sixth Crusade in 1228. He made a 10-year agreement with the Muslim leader al-Kamil to gain control of Jerusalem.

MAKE THE GRADE

More unsuccessful Crusades followed, but fewer and fewer people supported them. Many historians say the end of the Crusades was when Christians lost control of the city of Acre in 1291.

AFTER THE CRUSADES

Even after the Crusades, Muslims and Christians continued to fight. At the same time, the Muslim world introduced Europeans to new goods and foods, ideas about science, and even a way to make paper. The Crusades changed Europeans' way of life forever.

MUSLIM PAPERMAKING

MAKE THE GRADE

The Arabic number system (1, 2, 3, and so on) came from Muslims. It replaced Roman numerals in Europe.

A TIMELINE OF THE CRUSADES

1095
Pope Urban II orders Christians to capture Jerusalem.

1099
Jerusalem is captured by the Christians.

1145
The Second Crusade is called.

1187
Muslims led by Saladin capture Jerusalem.

1189
The Third Crusade begins.

1198
Pope Innocent III calls for the Fourth Crusade.

1204
Crusaders capture Constantinople.

1212
French and German children take part in the Children's Crusade.

1218
The Fifth Crusade begins.

1228
The Sixth Crusade begins.

1248
The Seventh Crusade begins.

1270
The Eighth Crusade begins.

1291
Muslims capture Acre, marking the end of the Crusades to many.

GLOSSARY

Asia Minor: the western part of Asia located mostly in the Asian part of Turkey

capture: to get control of

conquer: to take by force

expansion: the act of getting larger

Holy Roman Empire: an empire made up of German and Italian territories that existed from the 9th or 10th century to 1806

lance: a long, pointed weapon used in the past

Middle Ages: a time in European history from about 500 to 1500

preacher: a person who speaks publicly about religious subjects

prophet: a member of some religions who delivers messages that are believed to have come from God

religion: a belief in and way of honoring a god or gods

Roman numeral: one of the letters that were used by the ancient Romans to represent numbers and that are still used today

siege: the use of military to surround an area or building in order to capture it

FOR MORE INFORMATION

BOOKS

Kallen, Stuart A. *Life During the Crusades*. San Diego, CA: ReferencePoint Press, 2015.

Owen, Ruth. *The Life of a Medieval Knight*. New York, NY: AV2 by Weigl, 2018.

WEBSITES

Crusades
www.history.com/topics/crusades
Find out more about the battles of the Crusades.

The Crusades
www.bbc.com/education/guides/zjbj6sg/revision/1
Read more about the Crusades and their effect on the world.

INDEX